Animals I See at the Zoo

CHEETAHS

by Kathleen Pohl

Reading consultant: Susan Nations, M.Ed., author/literacy coach/
consultant in literacy development

WEEKLY READER®
PUBLISHING

Please visit our web site at: **www.garethstevens.com**
For a free color catalog describing our list of high-quality
books, call 1-800-542-2595 (USA) or 1-800-387-3178 (Canada).

Library of Congress Cataloging-in-Publication Data

Pohl, Kathleen.
    Cheetahs / Kathleen Pohl.
        p. cm. — (Animals I see at the zoo)
    Includes bibliographical references and index.
    ISBN 978-0-8368-8218-6 (lib. bdg.)
    ISBN 978-0-8368-8225-4 (softcover)
    1. Cheetah—Juvenile literature. I. Title.
QL737.C23P64   2007
599.75'9—dc22   2007006037

This edition first published in 2008 by
Weekly Reader® Books
An imprint of Gareth Stevens Publishing
1 Reader's Digest Road
Pleasantville, NY 10570-7000 USA

Copyright © 2008 by Gareth Stevens, Inc.

Editor: Dorothy L. Gibbs
Art direction: Tammy West
Graphic designer: Charlie Dahl
Photo research: Diane Laska-Swanke

Photo credits: Cover © G. Ronald Austing/Photo Researchers, Inc.; title © Photos.com; p. 5
© Lynda Richardson/CORBIS; p. 7 © Simon King/naturepl.com; pp. 9, 13 © Tom and Pat Leeson;
p. 11 © Joe McDonald/Visuals Unlimited; p. 15 © Tom Walker/Visuals Unlimited; p. 17 © T. J.
Rich/naturepl.com; p. 19 © Anup Shah/naturepl.com; p. 21 © Andrew Lichtenstein/CORBIS

Printed in the United States of America

1 2 3 4 5 6 7 8 9 11 10 09 08 07

Note to Educators and Parents

Reading is such an exciting adventure for young children! They are beginning to integrate their oral language skills with written language. To encourage children along the path to early literacy, books must be colorful, engaging, and interesting; they should invite the young reader to explore both the print and the pictures.

The *Animals I See at the Zoo* series is designed to help children read about the fascinating animals they might see at a zoo. In each book, young readers will learn interesting facts about the featured animal.

Each book is specially designed to support the young reader in the reading process. The familiar topics are appealing to young children and invite them to read — and re-read — again and again. The full-color photographs and enhanced text further support the student during the reading process.

In addition to serving as wonderful picture books in schools, libraries, homes, and other places where children learn to love reading, these books are specifically intended to be read within an instructional guided reading group. This small group setting allows beginning readers to work with a fluent adult model as they make meaning from the text. After children develop fluency with the text and content, the books can be read independently. Children and adults alike will find these books supportive, engaging, and fun!

— Susan Nations, M.Ed., author, literacy coach, and consultant in literacy development

I like to go to the zoo. I see **cheetahs** at the zoo.

Cheetahs are big cats. Their fur has lots of spots!

The spots help cheetahs hide in tall grass.

Cheetahs hunt during the day. They hunt for rabbits, deer, and other **prey**.

They have long legs and strong **claws**. Cheetahs can run very fast!

The black lines on a cheetah's face look like tears. Do you see them? They keep sunlight out of the cheetah's eyes.

tear lines

A baby cheetah has soft gray fur on the back of its head and neck. This fur goes away as the **cub** gets older.

Cheetahs lick themselves and each other to clean their fur.

I like to see
cheetahs at the
zoo. Do you?

Glossary

cheetahs — big cats with spotted fur that can run faster than any other land animals

claws — the hard, sharp "toenails" on a cat's paws

cub — another name for baby and young cheetahs

lick — to move the tongue over something with a rubbing motion

prey — an animal that is hunted for food

For More Information

Books

Clarke, Ginjer L. *Cheetah Cubs*. New York: Grosset & Dunlap, 2007.

Eckart, Edana. *Cheetahs*. New York: Scholastic, 2005.

Levine, Michelle. *Speedy Cheetahs*. Minneapolis: Lerner, 2006.

Vogel, Elizabeth. *Big Cats: Cheetahs*. New York: Rosen, Powerkids Press, 2002.

Web Site

National Geographic Kids: Creature Feature

www.nationalgeographic.com/kids/ creature_feature/0003/cheetah.html

Find fun facts, pictures, a video, a map, and a quiz.

Publisher's note to educators and parents: Our editors have carefully reviewed this Web site to ensure that it is suitable for children. Many Web sites change frequently, however, and we cannot guarantee that a site's future contents will continue to meet our high standards of quality and educational value. Be advised that children should be closely supervised whenever they access the Internet.

Index

About the Author

Kathleen Pohl has written and edited many children's books, including animal tales, rhyming books, retold classics, and the forty-book series *Nature Close-Ups*. Most recently, she authored the Weekly Reader® leveled reader series *Let's Read About Animals* and *Where People Work*. She also served for many years as top editor of *Taste of Home* and *Country Woman* magazines. She and her husband, Bruce, share their home in the beautiful Wisconsin woods with six goats, a llama, and all kinds of wonderful woodland creatures.